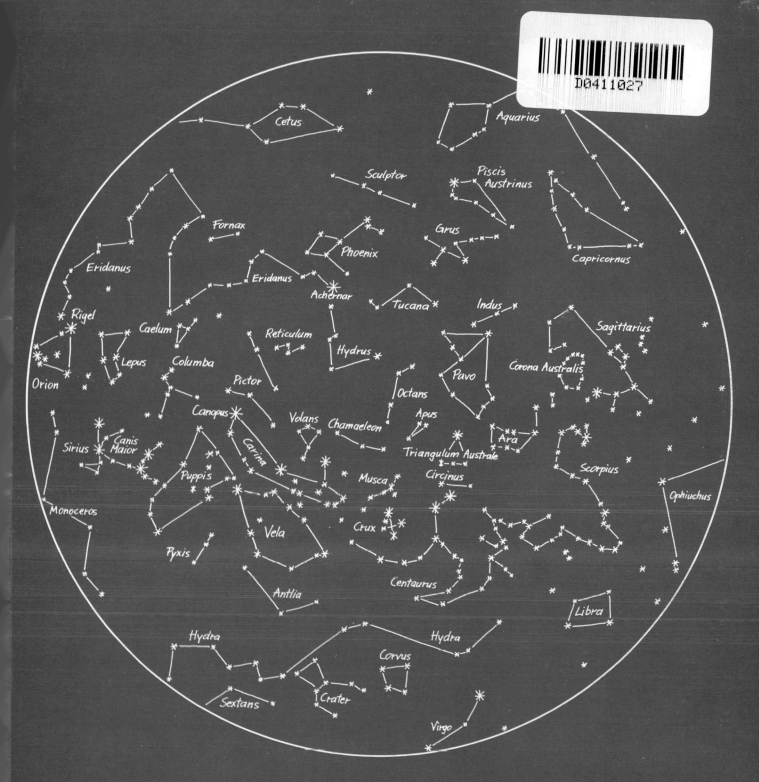

Southern hemisphere

Northern crown / *Corvus* Crow / *Crater* Cup / *Crux* Southern cross / *Cygnus* Swan / *Delphinus* Dolphin / *Draco* Dragon / *Equuleus* Foal / *Eridanus* River / *Fornax* Furnace / *Gemini* Twins / *Grus* Crane / *Hydra* Water serpent / *Hydrus* Water snake / *Indus* American Indian / *Lacerta* Lizard / *Leo* Lion / *Leo minor* Little lion / *Lepus* Hare / *Libra* Scales / *Lyra* Lyre / *Monoceros* Unicorn / *Musca* Fly / *Octans* Octant / *Ophiuchus* Serpent holder / *Pavo* Peacock / *Pictor* Painter's easel / *Pisces* Fish / *Piscis Austrinus* Southern fish / *Puppis* Stern / *Pyxis* Compass box / *Reticulum* Net / *Sagitta* Arrow / *Sagittarius* Archer / *Scorpius* Scorpion / *Sculptor* Sculptor's workshop / *Serpens* Serpent / *Sextans* Sextant / *Taurus* Bull / *Triangulum* Triangle / *Triangulum Australe* Southern triangle / *Tucana* Toucan /*Ursa major* Great bear / *Ursa minor* Little bear / *Vela* Sail / *Virgo* Virgin / *Volans* Flying fish.

For Caspar and Judith

The man who wrote this book and drew the pictures is not an expert at writing for children or a professional artist. He's an astronomer – someone who studies the stars and the universe. Here is a photograph of him. On the opposite page you can see a picture he drew. It shows what he used to dream about when he was a boy.

How far away are the Stars?

Discovering Astronomy

by Peppo Gavazzi

translated by Jacqueline Mitton

Cambridge University Press
Cambridge
New York   New Rochelle   Melbourne   Sydney

A first look
at the night sky

On a clear, dark night, the sky seems to be full of more stars than you can count. The brightest ones stand out as soon as you look up but most of the stars are so faint that you have to search the sky carefully if you want to see them. When the Moon is shining, the

sky is not very dark and you can
see far fewer stars. It's impossible
to see the faint stars because of the
moonlight. You can only see the
brightest ones.

How far away are the stars?

When I look out of my window at night, the sky looks like a big, black dome. The stars are scattered all over it. They seem to stay up there by magic. There's no string or anything else to hold them up.

The dome of the sky must be very big because I can't tell where it ends even if I go outside into the garden. Perhaps it covers the whole world.

In summer, I like to lie on the beach as night falls. The sky looks as if it plunges into the sea, a long, long way off. But it's no different from the sky I can see from my bedroom window at home. When I go up to the mountains, the sky is wonderfully clear. But it's still the same sky as over the town where I live.

Someone told me that I would still see the same sky if I went all the way to the United States of America. But America is so far away that I can hardly imagine it. I would need to sail across the sea for a long time to get there.

So, if the sky is so far away that it looks the same over the mountains as it does in America, then just how far away are the stars?

I talk to an astronomer

I really want to find out how far away the stars are. I ask my father but he doesn't know the answer. My teacher can't tell me either. The only way to find out is to ask a real astronomer. I go to see him in his office. There are lots of things on his desk and on the walls. Here are some of them:

① photographs of the sky
② a writing pad covered with notes
③ a reference book
④ a calculator
⑤ a magnifying glass
⑥ a pair of compasses
⑦ two pipes
⑧ some pages from a magazine
⑨ a pile of books and journals
⑩ a photograph of a skier in the mountains
⑪ a photograph of a group of people at a meeting
⑫ a blackboard with lines and symbols all over it
⑬ a picture of a sailing boat
⑭ a briefcase
⑮ photographs of an observatory and a big telescope
⑯ a photograph of the planet Saturn
⑰ a big metal filing cabinet that has pictures all over it, held on by little magnets.

I'm sure that he doesn't use all these things for his work. I suppose some of them are there just because

he likes to have them around. I think this astronomer must be an ordinary kind of person really.

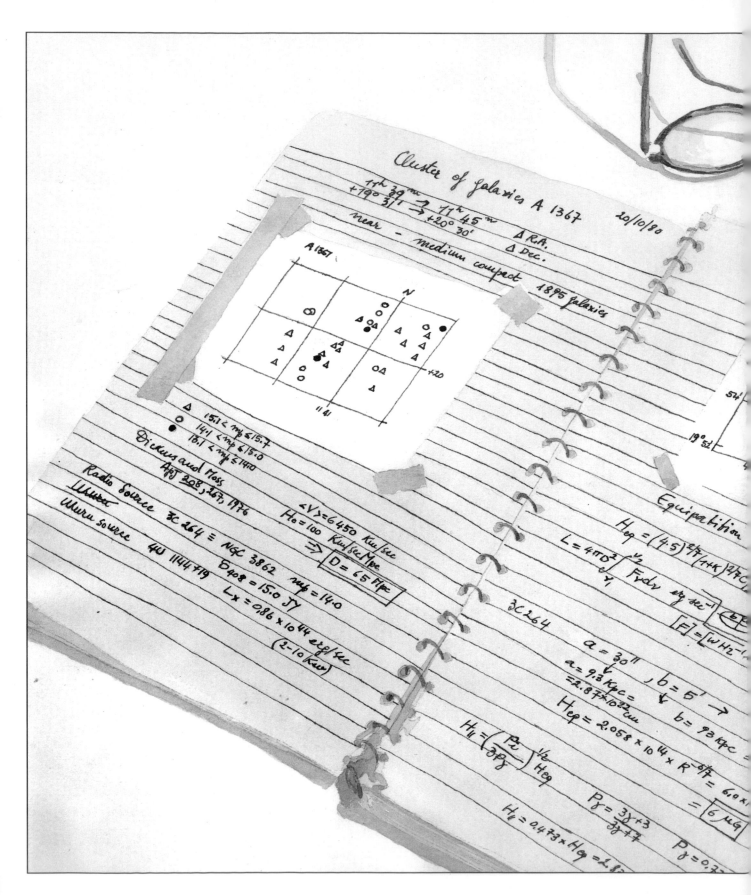

Look at what I've found – the astronomer's notebook! I can't understand a thing he's written. What do all these strange symbols and letters mean? The only thing that makes sense to me is a little boat in the top right-hand corner. I could draw one as good as that.

I wonder if he'll be able to tell me how far away the stars are? Will I understand what he says? But here he comes now.

'I'm very pleased you've come to see me', he says. 'It's a great idea. So, you'd like to know how far the stars are from the Earth? Well, I'll try to answer your question but not here in my office. Come with me and see what astronomers do. Tonight we'll go to the observatory. It's about fifty kilometres from here. The observatory has to be outside town because big telescopes need to be well away from the city lights. So, that's where we have to go.'

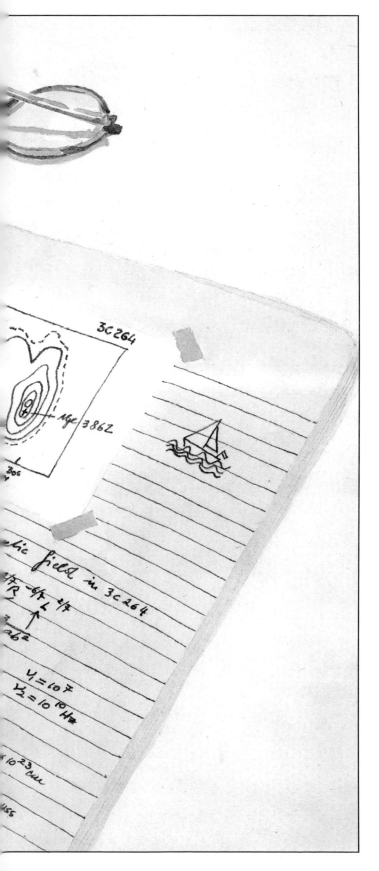

A night at the telescope

This large telescope is at an observatory in Chile in South America.

We have to climb up a spiral staircase to get into the dome of the observatory. Someone is already working there. *My* astronomer talks to me quietly so that he won't disturb the other person.

'I think that the best nights for looking at stars are winter nights. They are longer and often clearer than in summer. That means I can observe many more stars. On the other hand, they are the coldest nights. When the dome is open to the dark night sky and the shining stars, an icy wind blows in as well. It chills your bones and scatters your papers about.'

My astronomer is wearing a thick jacket and warm socks but he can't wear gloves. Gloves would make it difficult for him to turn the pages of his books, write down what he has seen and press the buttons that control the telescope. The night is so dark and quiet, I feel a little bit frightened. We don't talk very much. We don't like to break the mysterious silence. At daybreak, the astronomer closes the dome of the observatory. He would like to observe another star but he is quite glad to go to bed now.

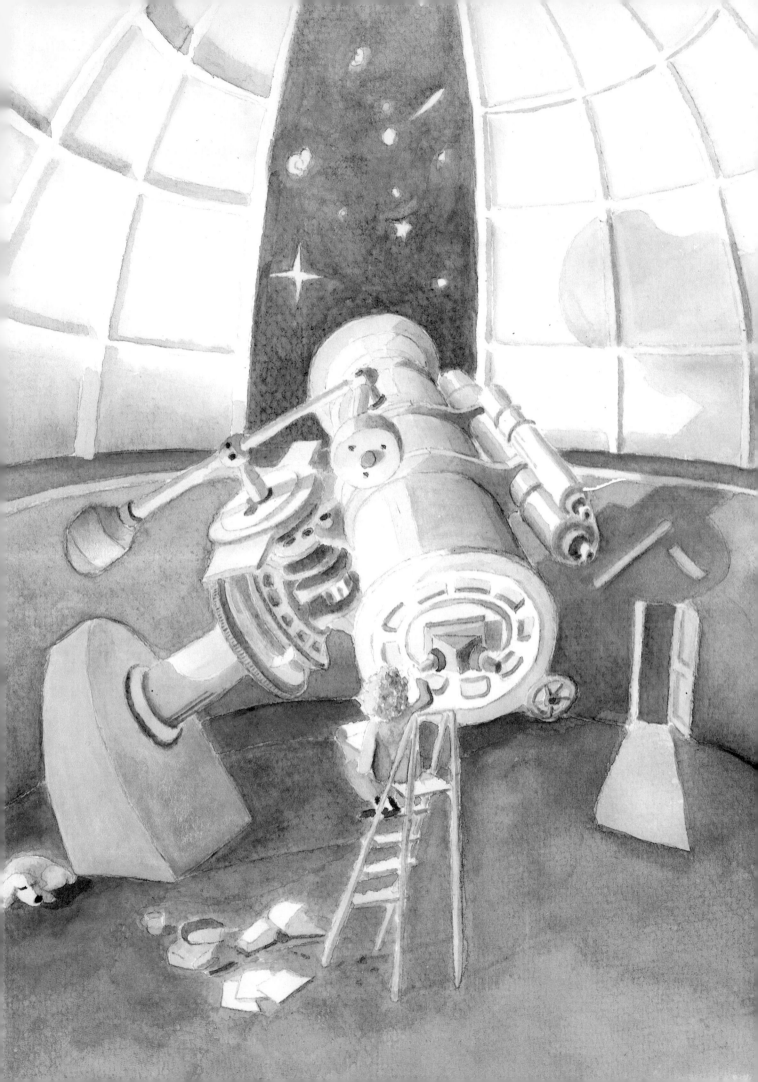

How to make things look bigger

'When you look at something through a telescope, it seems to be bigger. You might be looking at a ship out at sea. As it gets nearer, you may be able to see only part of it. But you'll be able to tell if there's anyone standing on the deck or what flag is flying.

'You can look at all kinds of things through a telescope – a small bird, if it's not too far away, or a whole skyscraper, if it's not too close. Then you can look at things in the sky like the Moon, or even whole galaxies, which are very far away indeed. But when you look at stars through a telescope, you can never tell how big they are or how far away.'

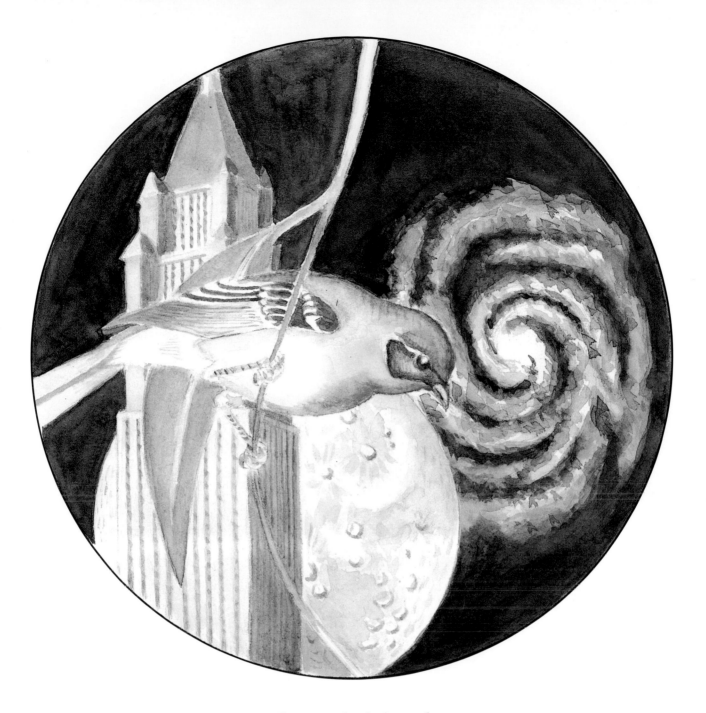

When you look through a
telescope, something that is small
and near can seem as big as
something that is much larger but
further away.

Black stars in a white sky?

The astronomer shows me a photograph of the sky. He has marked some stars by writing letters next to them. The oddest thing about this photograph is that the sky is white and the stars are little dark specks! The astronomer explains:

'First we take ordinary photographs with the telescope which show white stars in a dark sky. But it helps me to pick out the stars more easily to study them if the photograph is reversed like this.'

I can understand what he says. But a white sky still looks very strange to me. It isn't nearly as beautiful and mysterious as the night sky outside.

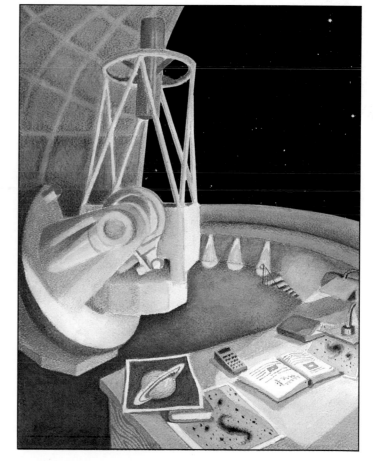

Here are two photographs of the same part of the sky. The top one is a normal photograph; the sky is black and the stars are white. Below it is the same photograph in reverse. It's easier to see the black dots and to mark them against the light background.

Observing the stars by day

'You can look at the sky at anytime, whether the Sun is shining or not, though you can only see the stars when it's dark and clear. But there are special telescopes, called *radiotelescopes* that can observe the stars even in daylight.

All the dishes of this big radiotelescope are pointing at the same part of the sky to make the map you can see on the opposite page.

Radiotelescopes don't take photographs – either ordinary ones or reversed ones. Instead, they draw pictures with lines, waves and spikes on them.'
The astronomer explains:
    'We can see stars and galaxies because they send out light. Some of them send out invisible radio waves as well as light.
A radiotelescope collects the radio waves, just like aerials on the roofs of houses collect signals sent out from radio and television stations. A computer inside the radiotelescope decodes these signals and turns them into a pattern like the one you can see here.

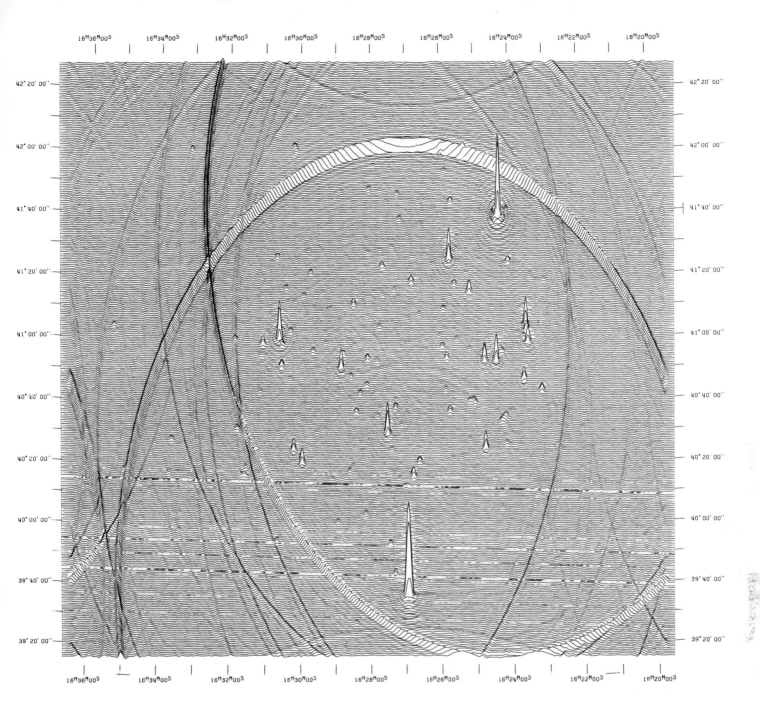

'Now that you've seen the astronomer's tools, we must go back to my office. Before I can explain how far away the stars are, I'll have to draw you some pictures.'

This is what the sky looks like when it's drawn by the computer of a radiotelescope. You can see lots of objects that send out radio waves. They show up as spikes.

How to draw the Earth

'You can draw anything you like on a piece of paper, even very big things. You can even fit the whole world onto one page in an atlas. Let's have a look at how a map like this is made.

'Before a house is built, the architect draws a plan. On this plan, the house is much smaller than it will really be. The plan won't have all the details on it.

'Suppose the next thing you want to do is to make a plan of the town where the house is going to be built. You will have to start again and draw everything smaller. If you don't, the town plan will end up as big as your house! On this town plan, the houses will be tiny squares that you can only just see.

'If you then want to make a map of the country that the town is in, you have to draw the villages as little dots and the wide rivers as thin lines.

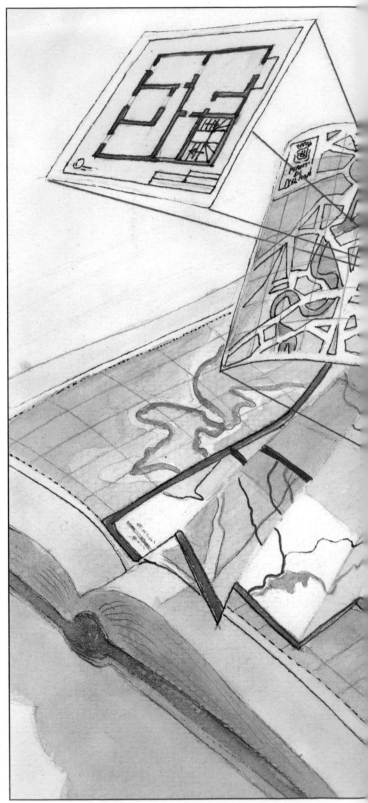

A photograph of part of the Earth taken by the spacecraft Gemini II. You can see India and Sri Lanka.

'Then imagine that you are going to draw a map of the whole continent that the country is in, with its thousands of towns and millions of houses. You will need to draw everything much smaller again.

'If you make everything on a map smaller by exactly the same amount, we say that the plan or map is *to scale*. The smaller you draw everything, the smaller the scale is.'

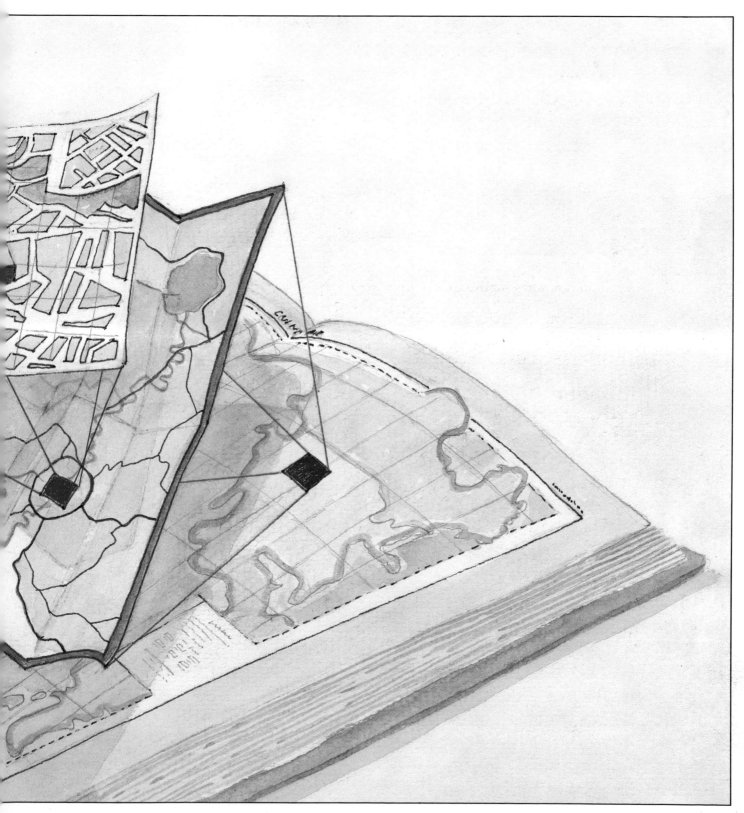

How to draw outer space

'You've seen how much smaller you have to make things if you're going to draw the whole world. Just imagine how small the scale has to be for drawing the stars and planets. Let's try it out.

'For a start, I'll draw the solar system – the Sun, Earth and the other planets. I'll make them fit on a large postage stamp. At that scale, the nearest stars are about ten metres from the Sun, so it's not going to work.

'I'll have to draw the stars at a smaller scale on another piece of paper. But if I want to draw our whole Galaxy – the Milky Way with all its stars – I'll have to start again with a much bigger piece of paper. In this picture, the solar system would be no more than a tiny point that you can hardly see.

'But our Galaxy isn't the only one. There are lots of other galaxies too. If I wanted to put the galaxies nearest ours on my picture as well, I would need a piece of paper a hundred times bigger. I don't have a piece that big, so I'll have to make the scale much smaller again. You see, it's impossible to fit the whole of space on a picture like this. The planets, stars and galaxies are too far apart. Astronauts have travelled as far as the Moon but people don't live long enough to journey all the way to the stars.

'Let's make an imaginary journey through space. First, we'll visit the nearest objects. Then we'll go further and further into the universe, as far as the most distant galaxies.'

Shooting stars

'Have you ever seen shooting stars flash across the sky on a summer night? No, they're not real stars that have got lost! They're really bits of rock travelling incredibly fast through space. When they hit the Earth's atmosphere, the air slows them down. Because they travel so fast, they get very hot and glow. They usually burn up completely. All we see is the bright trail in the sky that only lasts a few moments. If the rock does reach the ground, it will make a crater if it is big enough. We call these rocks *meteorites*. The planets are being hit by meteorites all the time.

'There are lots of craters made by meteorites on the Moon. You can see them easily through a small telescope. The Moon doesn't have an atmosphere, so all the meteorites that cross its path hit the ground at full speed. Only the biggest meteorites land on Earth. All the others are burnt up in the layer of air surrounding the Earth before they get there. We're lucky that the Earth has an atmosphere!

'So, shooting stars, or meteors, are not very far away – just a few kilometres above our heads.'

The Moon

'I'm sure you must have been out when the Moon is shining. Moonlight is not very bright at all. In fact, the Moon doesn't send out any light of its own. It reflects the light of the Sun. If the Sun didn't light up the Moon we wouldn't be able to see it.

'In the same way that the Earth goes round the Sun, the Moon goes round the Earth. On average, the Moon is 387,500 kilometres away from the Earth. That isn't really a very great distance compared with the size of the universe – only about ten times the distance round the Earth.

The Moon can sometimes be seen during the day.

The Earth rising over the Moon. This photograph was taken by the spacecraft, Apollo 11.

The Moon rising over the Earth.

24

'Many spacecraft have been sent
to the Moon and astronauts have
landed on it. It was the trip of a
lifetime for them and, when they
were on the Moon, they could look
at the Earth in the sky, exactly as
we see the Moon in our sky.'

The planets

'As far as we know, the Sun is the only star that has a family of nine planets going round it. Each one travels around the Sun in its own orbit and is lit by sunlight. In this picture, the lines that look like bits of string holding the planets up show how far each one is from the Sun.

'The Earth is about 150 million kilometres from the Sun. Mercury and Venus are nearer. Pluto is forty times further away.

'On the Earth, sunlight can be quite strong. You can feel its heat, especially in summer. If you stay out in the Sun all day, you have to be careful not to get burnt. If you lived on Mercury, you would be bright red in next to no time! It's much hotter on Mercury because the Sun is so close.

'On Pluto, you would need to stay in the Sun for about four years before you started to get burnt. Measuring distances by how sunburnt you get is an unusual way of comparing distances, isn't it?

'In this picture, the planets are drawn at a much bigger scale than the distances between them because otherwise the picture would be too big to fit in the book or else the planets would have to be tiny dots. I have drawn them so you can compare their sizes. Jupiter is the biggest. Next come Saturn, Uranus and Neptune. All the other planets, including Earth, are very much smaller.

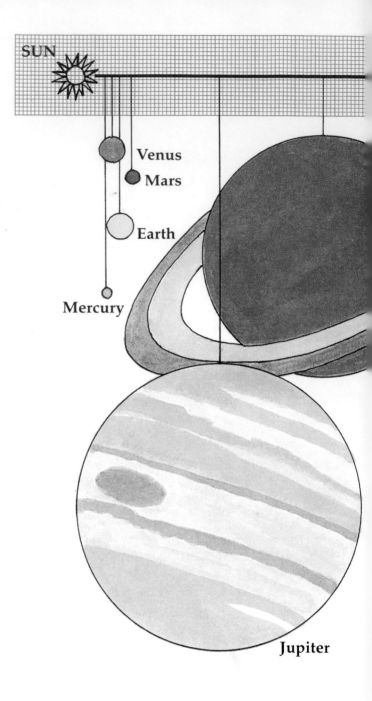

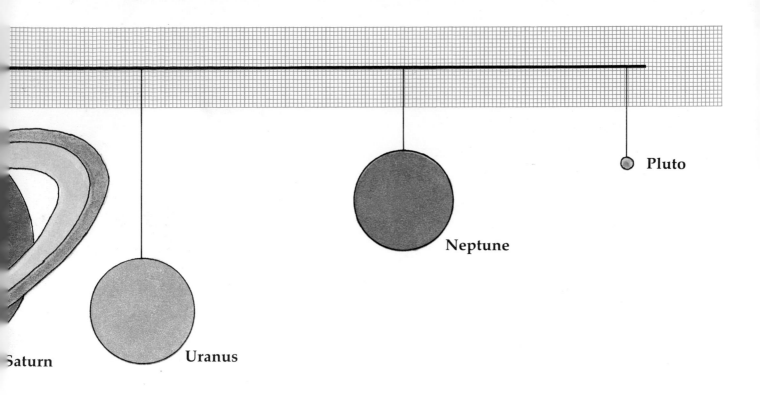

Saturn

Uranus

Neptune

Pluto

'I could tell you how far the planets are from the Sun in kilometres but the numbers are so huge that you probably wouldn't get any real idea of just how far away they really are. So here is another way of judging the distances – by roughly how long it might take you to get sunburn on each planet.'

Mercury	2 hours
Venus	6 hours
Earth	12 hours
Mars	2 days
Jupiter	1 month
Saturn	3 months
Uranus	1 year
Neptune	2½ years
Pluto	4 years

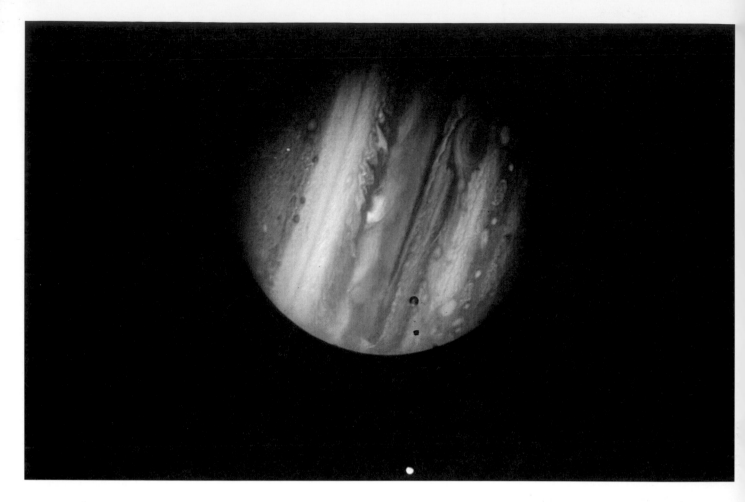

Jupiter

'These are photographs of Jupiter,
the biggest planet in the Sun's
family. They were taken from a
spacecraft that had a television
camera on board. The spacecraft
took a year and a half to get to
Jupiter. It only took the astronauts
who went to the Moon three days
to get there.

'You can see Jupiter's Great Red
Spot. Astronomers have known
about it for a long time. From these
photographs they think it's a giant
hurricane but nobody knows why it
has been blowing for hundreds of
years or why it's red.'

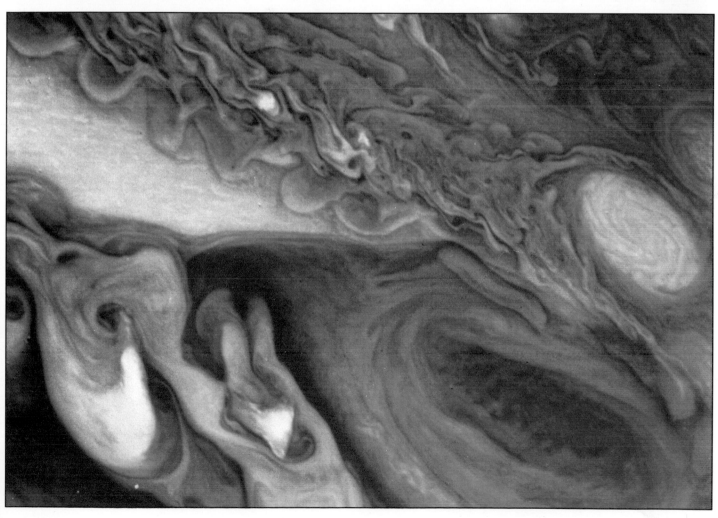

This photograph of Comet Humason was taken in 1961 at one of the large observatories in the United States.

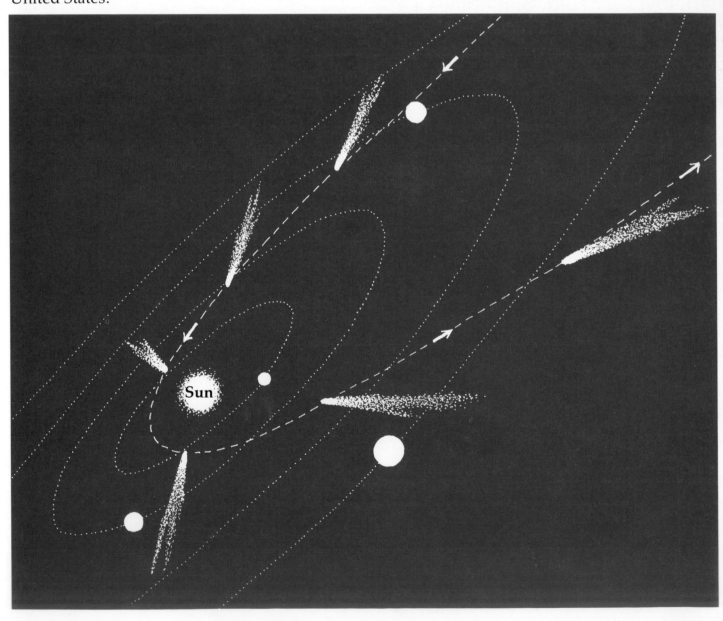

This little picture shows where a comet's tail would point if there wasn't any solar wind. The bottom picture on the page opposite shows what actually happens.

Comets

'Comets are not like stars or planets. They're clumps of ice, gas and dust. They go in orbits around the Sun, but a very long way away where it's icy cold. Sometimes a comet gets near to the Sun. Then the Sun's heat makes the comet give off gas and dust. This gas and dust makes the comet's tail.

'Astronomers have found out that the tail of a comet always points away from the Sun, like a flag blown by a fan. This means that when a comet is travelling away from the Sun, its tail streams in front of it! Imagine a steam train with the smoke blowing forwards in the direction the train is going. So from looking at comets, we know that the Sun acts just like a fan. What astronomers call the *solar wind* blows in all directions away from the Sun.'

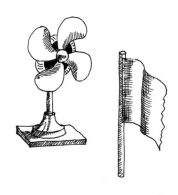

The Sun

The Sun is a star like all the other stars. It's the only star we can see in the day, because it's so close to the Earth. Without the Sun there would be no life on Earth – there would be no light and no warmth.

'Like all the stars, the Sun is a ball of shining, hot gas. But there are some places on the Sun that don't shine as brightly as the rest. They are called sunspots and they look like small, dark patches.

'Remember, NEVER LOOK STRAIGHT AT THE SUN, either with or without a telescope. It's *very dangerous*. You will hurt your eyes badly and could even blind yourself. The only really safe way to observe the Sun is to project an image of it onto a piece of white paper. You can do this through a telescope or through a tiny hole in the blinds of a dark room.'

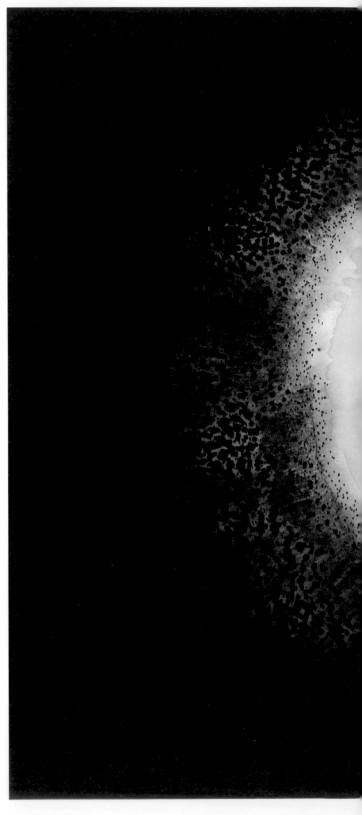

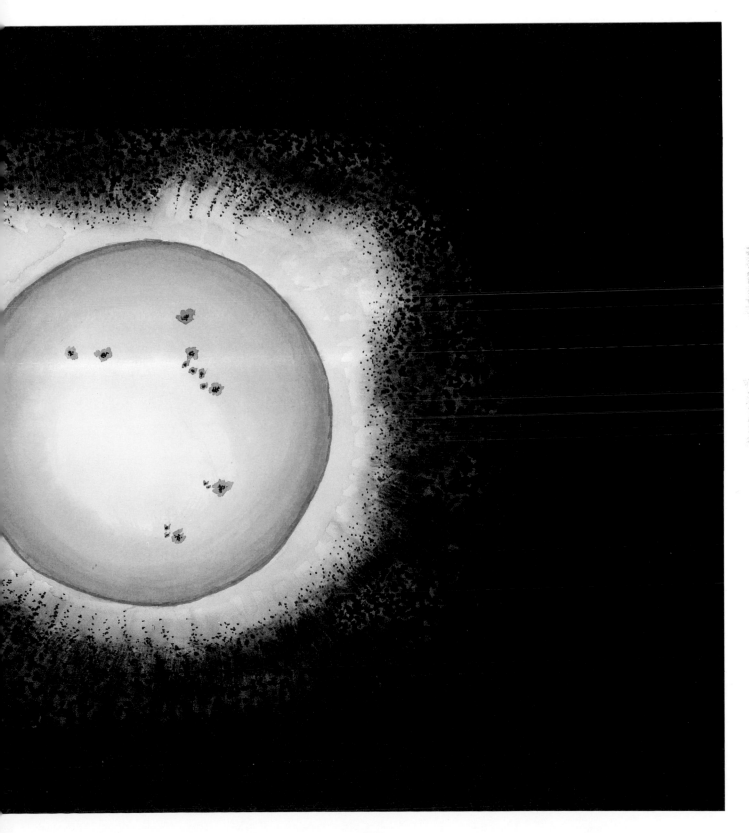

The Pleiades

'On a clear, winter night, you can see the star cluster called the Pleiades without a telescope. It looks like a bunch of grapes hanging in the sky. Through a telescope you can see even more stars. They're surrounded by faint blue clouds of misty light that make them look rather mysterious. These haloes are clouds of dust and gas that reflect the starlight.

'Compared with the Sun, the Pleiades are a long way away. But astronomers think they're quite near because they're used to studying things even further away.'

You can find the Pleiades by starting from the constellation Orion, which is fairly easy to spot. From Orion, look upwards and to the right until you can see the constellation Taurus. The Pleiades are above Taurus and to the right.

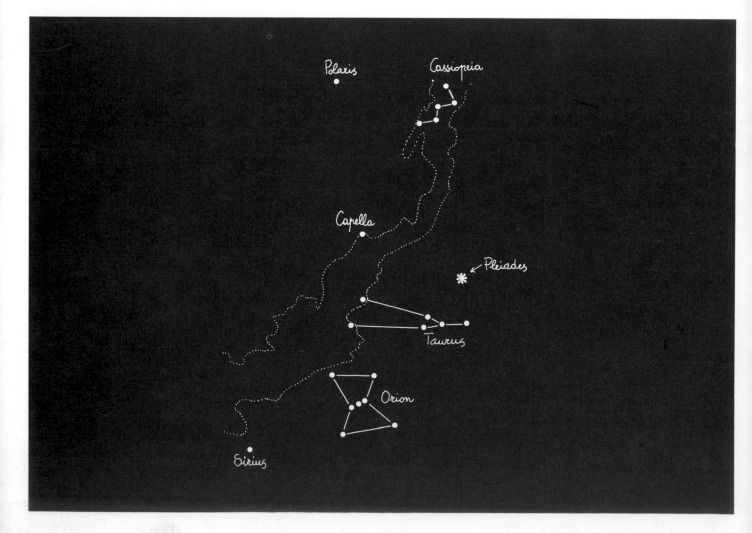

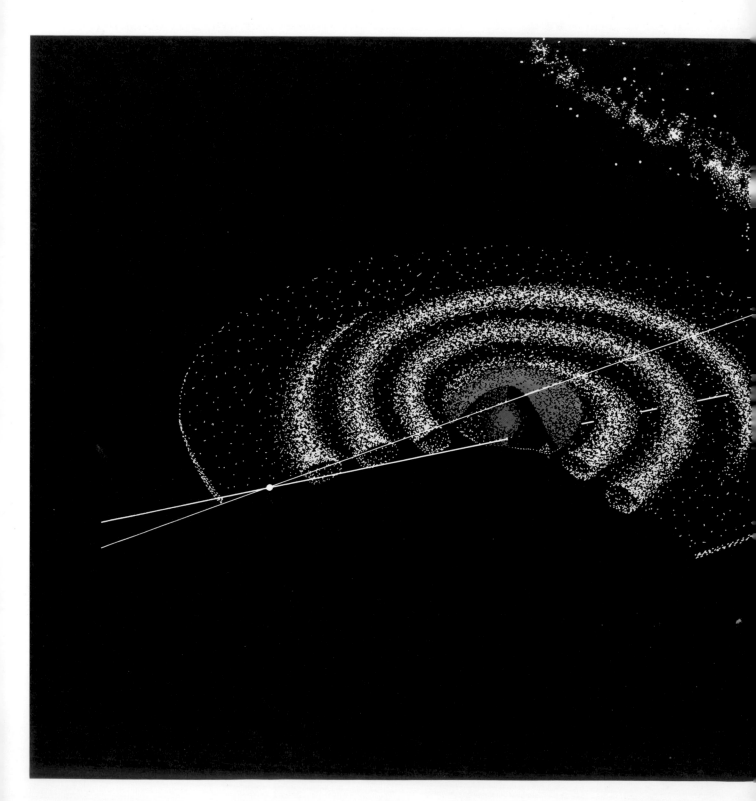

'To see the Milky Way, go out on a clear, dark, summer night. You need to get away from the city lights and traffic. When all you can see is the stars, you will get a clear view of the Milky Way.

'The Milky Way is a faint band of light that circles the whole sky. If you can look at it with a telescope, you will see that it's made up of countless stars.

'Astronomers have found out that the Milky Way Galaxy is flat and round, like a plate. The distance across this starry disc is about a thousand times greater than its thickness. Many galaxies look like this. But why does the Milky Way look like a band round the sky to us? The reason is that we live inside it. The white dot in the picture shows where the Sun's family (including the Earth) is in the Galaxy. You can see we are a long way from the centre. The white band of stars on the right of the picture is what we see in the sky because we are looking through the Galaxy. If we could go and look at our Galaxy from above, we would see that it has a spiral shape.'

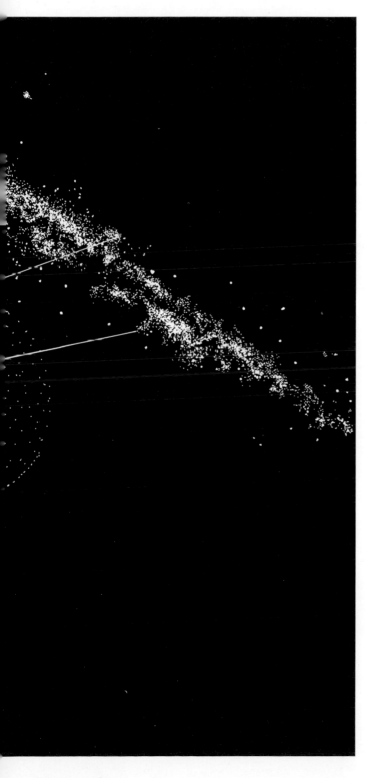

The Andromeda Galaxy

'If we could see the Milky Way from the outside, it would look a bit like the photograph on the opposite page. But this isn't a photograph of the Milky Way. It's the Andromeda Galaxy, one of the galaxies nearest to our own Galaxy. How close is it really? Well, it takes a beam of light from the Andromeda Galaxy more than two million years to reach the Earth.

'The Andromeda Galaxy is only just visible to us without a telescope. It looks like a fuzzy star because it's so far away. You need a very powerful telescope to take a photograph like the one here.'

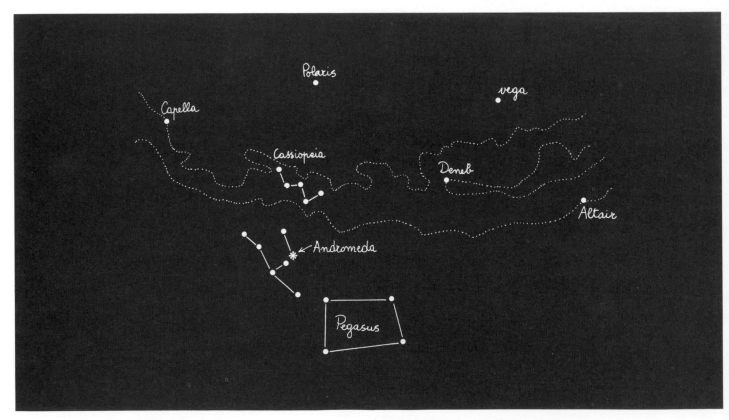

You can find Andromeda in the sky on a summer night below the constellation Cassiopeia. Cassiopeia has five bright stars making a w-shape and it's in the band of the Milky Way.

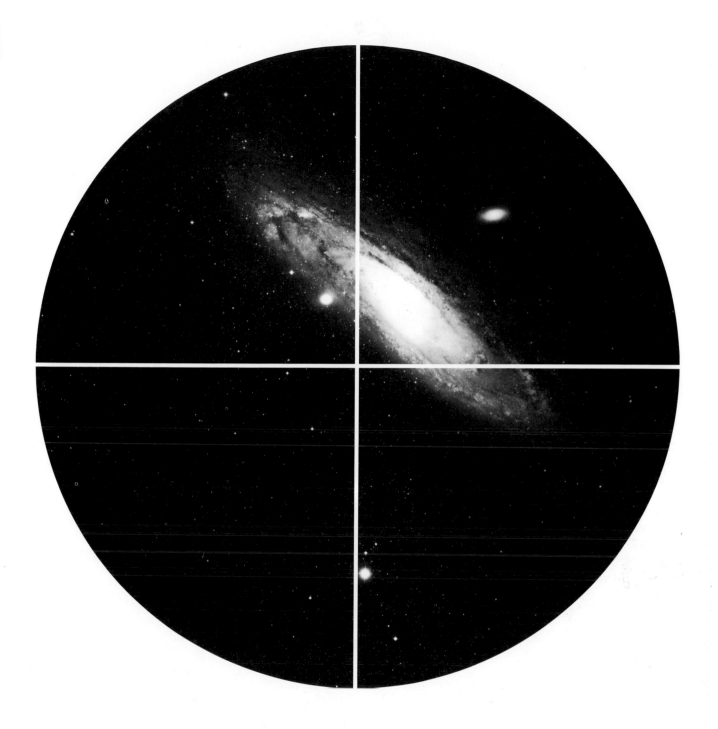

The universe goes on and on

Here are some photographs of galaxies. You can see some of the different shapes they can have.

'There are millions of other galaxies. Some are near to our own and the Andromeda Galaxy. Others are much further away. They come in different shapes. Some are spirals. Some are egg-shaped ones called elliptical galaxies. Others have no particular shape and are called irregular galaxies. I like them all, whatever they're called.

'Every galaxy contains billions of stars similar to the Sun. But most galaxies are so far away that you can't see the individual stars, even by using a very big telescope. That's how big the universe is and that's how far away the stars are.'

These six photographs are all of the same galaxy. The strange colours have been produced by a computer to help show up the things that interest astronomers.

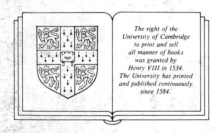

Published by the Press Syndicate of the University of Cambridge
The Pitt Building, Trumpington Street, Cambridge CB2 1RP
32 East 57th Street, New York, NY 10022, USA
10 Stamford Road, Oakleigh, Melbourne 3166, Australia

Originally published in German 1984 as *Wie weit ist der Himmel* by Otto Maier Verlag, Ravensburg
© 1984 Otto Maier Verlag, Ravensberg

First published in English by Cambridge University Press 1987 as *How far away are the Stars?*
English translation © Cambridge University Press 1987
Reprinted 1988

Printed in Hong Kong by Wing King Tong

British Library Cataloguing in Publication Data
Gavazzi, Peppo
How far away are the stars?: discovering astronomy.
1. Astronomy – Juvenile literature
I. Title   II. Wie weit ist der Himmel?
English
520   QB46

ISBN 0 521 35516 7

DS